# A Concise Lojong Manual

From:
Huei-Ling
Tel: 3161

ISBN: 978-0-9881762-6-3
Library of Congress Control Number: 2014932153

Bird of Paradise Press
1223 N. Lee Hwy, #250
Lexington, VA 24450 USA
birdofparadisepress.org

This is the third printing of this translation.
A previous edition of this book was published by
Marpa Kagyu Dharma Preservation Center
Kathmandu, Nepal, March 2010.
First United States edition, Bird of Paradise Press, 2014

Introduction and translation from Tibetan into English by Pamela Gayle White. Special thanks to Lodrö Rinpoché of the Marpa Kagyu Dharma Preservation Center who kindly gave us his permission to reprint this book.

Original front cover design and interior layout by Pamela Gayle White. Design adapted for the United States edition by Annie Heckman.

# A Concise Lojong Manual

Könchok Yenlak
the 5th Shamarpa

translated by Pamela Gayle White

Bird of Paradise Press
Lexington, VA

# Translator's introduction

This short lojong instruction manual by the 5th Shamarpa, Könchok Yenlak, contains the familiar root maxims as well as concise, pithy comments and explanations. Lojong–"mind training" in English–has become a popular subject for students and practitioners of Mahayana Buddhism. Numerous commentaries, both classic and contemporary, are available in many languages. This small text is not meant to replace them. Rather, we hope that it will be the sort of book one can slip into one's pocket and refer to when inspiration strikes. It might also be useful as a support for short lojong courses and retreats.

The original Tibetan text is given for reference. Words and phrases in brackets were added by the translator.

We have also included a brief introduction presenting the author of the commentary, Shamar Könchok Yenlak, gleaned from the *Golden Rosary of the Kagyu Lineage* and other texts with the help of Gen Lekshay Gyatso from Swayambhu, Nepal.

We offer our sincere apologies for all mistakes, and extend heartfelt thanks to scholars, proof-readers, typists, and the publisher. May this booklet be of some small benefit to fellow travelers feeling their way along the path.

Pamela Gayle White
Boudhanath, Nepal
March 2010

# About Shamar Könchok Yenlak

In the history of Tibetan Buddhism, the tradition of lineages headed by incarnate masters began in the early 13th century. The highly realized meditation master Düsum Khyenpa clearly announced his return in a letter given to his main disciple, Drogön Réchen. Thus his successor, Karma Pakshi, was a formally recognized *tulku* (སྤྲུལ་སྐུ), a word meaning "emanation body" or "re-incarnated master." Düsum Khyenpa and Karma Pakshi were the 1st and 2nd Karmapas: supreme heads of the Karma Kagyu Lineage, one of the four main schools of Tibetan Buddhism. The tradition they began has continued to the present day as an unbroken stream of realized guides who are recognized by their main disciples based on prophecies, prediction letters, or other, less apparent means.

The foremost disciple of the 3rd Karmapa, Rangjung Dorjé, was Khédroup Drakpa Sengé, the first Shamar Rinpoché. His title dates from the time when the 3rd Karmapa presented him with a ruby-red hat (*sha mar*/ཞྭ་དམར) which was a replica of his own black hat (*sha nak*/ཞྭ་ནག།), the birthright of the Karmapas. This gift of a crown symbolized the equal realization and activity of the Karmapa and his disciple, the Shamarpa.

According to his biographers, the 5th Shamarpa, Könchok Yenlak (1526–83), was born in a remote area of Tibet called Kyen Zhölmo Ché. While pregnant, his mother had many auspicious dreams, and everyone nearby could clearly hear the unborn child reciting Avalokita's six-syllable mantra *Om Mani Padmé Houng*. An unusually mature newborn, the baby could recognize his parents after only two or three days and was soon able to identify people he had been close to in his previous life. There are numerous stories of Könchok Yenlak's exceptional abilities during his early years.

When the child was two, the 8th Karmapa, Mikyö Dorjé (1507–1554), met with his father and asked that the boy be entrusted to him for ordination. After some discussion, the parents agreed to the Karmapa's request. The Karmapa gave their son his name, Könchok Yenlak: *Attribute of the Three Jewels*. Then he cut his hair and told his father to keep him in pure surroundings, as he would soon send for him. Two years later, emissaries came to take Könchok Yenlak to the Karmapa's monastery. When the child overheard their conversation with his parents, he laughed with evident delight and seemed eager to leave on the spot.

When the party arrived at the monastery, the Karmapa received them and declared that since it was obvious who the boy really was, the usual methods of examination were unnecessary. However, in order to convince and inspire others, he would have to undergo the generally accepted *tulku* recognition procedures. For example, the Karmapa presented the child with two statues, one of the 4th Karmapa Rölpé Dorjé and one of the 2nd Shamarpa Kachö Wangpo, and said: tell me which one is you! The boy immediately placed both statues on his head to receive their blessing. The Karmapa again said: now take *your* statue. Laughing merrily, the boy kept hold of Kachö Wangpo's statue, then touched his nose with his finger and said: look! This is me! Needless to say, he passed all tests with flying colors.

He was formally recognized and enthroned as the Shamarpa at the age of eight. At that time, Mikyö Dorjé gave him the name Könchok Bâng, *Subject of the Three Jewels*, and crowned him with the red hat of the Shamarpa lineage.

He spent some years with the Karmapa, receiving and practicing the fundamental teachings of the Karma Kagyu Lineage. The young Shamarpa also received the three levels of precepts from Mikyö Dorjé. When he was 22 years old, he entered retreat in a cave in the holy place of Tsari where he gained full realization of the nature of mind and phenomena.

Mikyö Dorjé, the 8th Karmapa, passed away when Shamar Könchok Yenlak was in his late 20s. A mystical song sung by the Karmapa when he was in retreat in Kongpo and entrusted to the Shamarpa clearly stated where to look for his successor. Recognition of the 9th Karmapa, Wangchouk Dorjé (1556–1603), was confirmed by Shamar Könchok Yenlak and Situ Chökyi Gocha. As the acting Karma Kagyu lineage holder, Shamar Rinpoché officially enthroned the Karmapa when he was six years old and gave him his name, Palden Mipham Chökyi Wangchouk. Könchok Yenlak was the 9th Karmapa's root lama.

Shamar Könchok Yenlak is remembered for his tireless bodhisattva activity. He built a number of monasteries and ordained his disciples with great enthusiasm. His footprint can be seen in a rock by the river near Dakpo Shédroup Ling in Tibet, where he went to offer colored mandala sand after some Tibetan New Year's celebrations. He composed many memorable treatises, notably on madhyamika, abhidharma, tantric practice, the six yogas of Naropa, mahamudra meditation, and Tibetan language. His collected works are generally presented in eight substantial volumes.

# A Concise Lojong Manual

༄༅། །བློ་སྦྱོང་གི་ཁྲིད་མདོར་བསྡུས་པ་བཞུགས།།

བླ་མ་དམ་པ་དང་བྱང་ཆུབ་ཀྱི་སེམས་རིན་པོ་ཆེ་ལ་སྐྱབས་སུ་མཆིའོ། །ཇོ་བོ་རྗེ་དཔལ་ལྡན་ཨ་ཏི་ཤས་བླ་མ་གསེར་གླིང་པ་ལ་གསན་པའི་བྱང་ཆུབ་སེམས་ཀྱི་བློ་སྦྱོང་གི་མན་ངག་འདི་ལ་ཁྲིད་ཚུལ་མི་འདྲ་བ་མང་དུ་ཡོད་ཀྱང་དགེ་བའི་བཤེས་གཉེན་འཆད་ཁ་བའི་ལུགས་ཀྱིས་དོན་བདུན་དུ་མཛད་དེ། སྔོན་འགྲོ་རྟེན་གྱི་ཆོས་བསྟན་པ། དངོས་གཞི་བྱང་ཆུབ་ཀྱི་སེམས་སྦྱོང་བ༑ རྐྱེན་ངན་བྱང་ཆུབ་ཀྱི་ལམ་དུ་བསྒྱུར་བ། ཚེ་གཅིག་གི་ཉམས་ལེན་དྲིལ་ནས་བསྟན་པ། བློ་འབྱོངས་པའི་ཚད། བློ་སྦྱོང་གི་དམ་ཚིག བློ་སྦྱོང་གི་བསླབ་བྱ་དང་བདུན་ནོ། །

I take refuge in the perfect lama and in the most precious mind of awakening. The glorious Dharma Lord Atisha received these key instructions on training in developing bodhicitta, the mind of awakening, from Lama Serlingpa.

Although there are many different teachings on the subject, this has been composed according to Spiritual Friend Chekawa's seven-point system.

The seven are:

- **The preliminaries: presenting the practitioner's basic Dharma teachings.**

- **The main practice: training in bodhicitta, awakening mind.**

- **Transforming adverse circumstances into the path of awakening.**

- **Explanations on incorporating the practice during one's lifetime.**

- **Evaluating progress in mind training.**

- **The mind training commitments.**

- **The mind training guidelines.**

དང་པོ་ནི།  དང་པོ་སྔོན་འགྲོ་དག་ལ་བསླབ།  ཅེས་
གསུངས་ཏེ་ད་ལན་གྱི་མི་ལུས་འདི་ལན་གཅིག་ཡིན་གྱི།
ཕྱིས་ནས་རྙེད་དཀའ་བར་བསམ།  འཆི་བ་ནམ་ཡོང་ཆ་མེད་
གློ་བུར་དུ་ཡོང་བར་བསམ།  འཁོར་བ་ཐམས་ཅད་སྡུག་
བསྔལ་དུ་བསམ།  མི་དགེ་བ་ལས་སྡུག་བསྔལ་དང་དགེ་བ་
ལས་བདེ་བ་འབྱུང་བར་བསམ་པ་རྣམས་སོ།  །

## The first point:
**First, train in the preliminaries.**

Consider the fact that although we now have a human body, it will be difficult to obtain one in the future.

Consider that the time of death is uncertain; it may arrive all of a sudden.

Consider that all cyclic existence entails suffering.

Consider that suffering originates in non-virtue, and happiness originates in goodness.

གཉིས་པ་དངོས་གཞི་བྱང་ཆུབ་ཀྱི་སེམས་གཉིས་སྦྱོང་བ་ལ། དོན་དམ་བྱང་སེམས་དང་། ཀུན་རྫོབ་བྱང་སེམས་སྦྱོང་བ་གཉིས། དང་པོ་ལ་སྦྱོར་བ་ནི། དངོས་སུ་འབྱོར་ན་ཡང་རུང་། དམིགས་པས་བསྒོམས་ཀྱང་རུང་སྟེ། བླ་མ་དཀོན་མཆོག་གི་མདུན་དུ། མ་ནམ་མཁའི་སྐྱབས་འགྲོ་བློ་མ་འགྱུར་བར་དུ་བྱས་། ཡན་ལག་བདུན་པ་ཕུལ་ནས། སེམས་བསྐྱེད་པར་བྱ་སྟེ། བྱང་ཆུབ་སྙིང་པོར་མཆིས་ཀྱི་བར། །སངས་རྒྱས་རྣམས་ལ་སྐྱབས་སུ་མཆི། །ཆོས་དང་བྱང་ཆུབ་སེམས་དཔའ་ཡི། །ཚོགས་ལའང་དེ་བཞིན་སྐྱབས་སུ་མཆི། །ཇི་ལྟར་སྔོན་གྱི་བདེ་གཤེགས་ཀྱིས། །བྱང་ཆུབ་ཐུགས་ནི་བསྐྱེད་པ་དང་། །བྱང་ཆུབ་སེམས་དཔའི་བསླབ་པ་ལ། །དེ་དག་རིམ་བཞིན་གནས་པ་ལྟར། དེ་བཞིན་འགྲོ་ལ་ཕན་དོན་དུ། །བྱང་ཆུབ་སེམས་ནི་བསྐྱེད་བགྱི་ཞིང་། །དེ་བཞིན་དུ་ནི་བསླབ་པ་ལའང་། །རིམ་པ་བཞིན་དུ་བསླབ་པར་བགྱི། །ཞེས་སྐྱབས་འགྲོ་སེམས་བསྐྱེད་བྱ། ལྷ་དང་བླ་མ་ལ་གསོལ་བ་གདབ། ཡན་ལག་བདུན་པ་རྒྱས་པར་ཕུལ་ནས་ལུས་དྲང་པོར་བསྲངས་ཏེ།

◈ **The second point, the main practice,** is training in developing both aspects of awakening mind: ultimate bodhicitta and conventional bodhicitta.

The preparation phase of the former, [ultimate bodhicitta,] takes place before the lama and the three jewels, whether materially present or visualized. Recite the 'Manam' refuge until the mind has been transformed, then offer a seven-branch prayer and develop bodhicitta thus:

*Until the heart of awakening has become manifest,*
*I take refuge in the buddhas.*
*Likewise, I take refuge in the Dharma and the assembly of bodhisattvas.*
*Just as the sugatas of the past cultivated awakening mind and progressively trained as bodhisattvas, stage by stage, for the sake of beings, I too will foster awakening mind and train just as they did, stage by stage.*

With this, practice refuge and bodhicitta, invoke the deities and lamas, and offer an extensive seven-branch prayer. Straighten your physical

དབུགས་ཕྱིར་འགྲོ་ནང་འགྲོ་ཉེར་གཅིག་གི་བར་མ་འཁྲུགས་པ་ལྷག་ཆད་མེད་པར་བགྲང་། དེས་བསམ་གཏན་གྱི་སྣོད་རུང་དུ་འགྱུར་རོ། །གཉིས་པ་དངོས་གཞི་ནི། ཆོས་རྣམས་རྨི་ལམ་ལྟ་བུར་བསམ། ཞེས་པས་སེམས་འཁྲུལ་པའི་སྣང་ཆ་མ་གཏོགས་ཕྱི་རོལ་ན་མེད་པར་བསམ། མ་སྐྱེས་རིག་པའི་གཤིས་ལ་དཔྱད། ཅེས་པས་སེམས་ཀྱང་སྐྱེ་འགག་གནས་གསུམ་དང་བྲལ་བར་བསམ། གཉེན་པོ་ཉིད་ཀྱང་རང་སར་གྲོལ༔ ཞེས་པས་ལྟ་སྒོམ་བྱེད་མཁན་གྱི་སེམས་དེ་ག་ལ་བལྟས་པས་དེ་ཡང་སྐྱེ་འགག་གནས་པ་དང་བྲལ་བ། ཁ་དོག་དང་དབྱིབས་མེད་པ། ལུས་ཀྱི་ཕྱི་ནང་གང་དུའང་མི་གནས་པ།

posture and breathe serenely in and out twenty-one times—no more, no less. This is how one becomes a suitable vessel for meditative stability.

The second phase [of training in ultimate bodhicitta] is the main one.

**Consider all phenomena as dreams.**

Consider that they are nothing more than the mind's confused projections and do not exist outside of it.

**Examine the unborn nature of awareness.**

Consider that mind is also free of beginning, cessation and dwelling.

**The remedy too liberates itself naturally.**

Look at the very mind of that person who is watching and meditating: it too is free of beginning, cessation, and dwelling. Colorless and formless, it does not reside anywhere in or out of the body; it has no innate nature. Therefore, settle in a thought-free state without any intellectual grasping whatsoever.

གཞིས་ཅིར་མ་གྲུབ་པ་དེ་ལ་བློས་ཅིར་ཡང་མི་འཛིན་པར་རྟོག་
མེད་ཀྱི་ངང་དུ་བཞག་གོ །དེའི་འཇོག་ཚུལ་ནི། ལམ་གྱི་
ངོ་བོ་ཀུན་གཞིའི་ངང་ལ་བཞག །ཅེས་པ་དེའོ། །གསུམ་
པ་རྗེས་ཀྱི་ཉམས་ལེན་ནི། ཐུན་མཚམས་སྒྱུ་མའི་སྐྱིས་བུར་བྱ།
ཞེས་པས་ཆོས་ཐམས་ཅད་རང་བཞིན་མེད་པ་སྒྱུ་མ་ལྟ་བུར་ཤེས་
པར་བྱས་ནས་ཟས་གོས་གནས་མལ་དགྲ་གཉེན་སོགས་གང་ལ་
ཡང་ཞེན་པ་མེད་པར་བྱའོ། །གཉིས་པ་ཀུན་རྫོབ་བྱང་སེམས་
སྦྱོང་བ་ལ། མཉམ་བཞག་དང་རྗེས་ཐོབ་གཉིས།

As for how to settle, it is said that:

**The essence of the path is to settle in the nature of alaya, the ground of all experience.**

The third phase [of training in ultimate bodhicitta] is the post-meditation practice.

**Between sessions, be someone who is in tune with illusion.**

Once you have realized that all phenomena are inherently non-existent and illusion-like, be without any yearnings regarding food, clothing, home, friends, enemies, and so on.

The second aspect [of the second main point, training in bodhicitta, awakening mind] is training in relative bodhicitta during meditation and afterwards.

དང་པོ་ནི། གཏོང་ལེན་གཉིས་པོ་སྤེལ་མར་སྦྱངས། ཞེས་པས་སེམས་ཅན་ཐམས་ཅད་རང་གི་མ་ཡིན་པའི་བྱམས་པ་དང་། དེ་རྣམས་ད་ལྟར་སྡུག་བསྔལ་བ་ལ་སྙིང་རྗེ་དྲག་ཏུ་སྒོམ། མ་ལ་གང་གིས་གནོད་ན་སྡུག་བསྔལ་དང་ཉོན་མོངས་པས་གནོད་པས༑ དེ་ཐམས་ཅད་རང་གི་སྙིང་ནང་དུ་བླང་བར་བསྒོམ་ཞིང་། བླང་ན་དགའ་བའི་འདུན་པ་དྲག་ཏུ་བྱ། མ་ལ་ཅིས་ཕན་ན་བདེ་བ་དང་དགེ་བས་ཕན་པས། རང་གི་བདེ་དགེ་ཐམས་ཅད་མ་ལ་ཐིམ་པས་མ་དེ་འཕྲལ་དུ་བདེ་ཞིང་ཆོས་སྒྲུབ་པའི་རྐྱེན་ཚང་ནས་འཚང་རྒྱ་ནུས་སུ་བསྒོམ། དེ་གཉིས་རླུང་ལ་བསྐྱོན་པར་བྱ༑ ཞེས་པས་རླུང་ཚུར་རྔུབ་དུས་སེམས་ཅན་གྱི་སྡིག་སྡུག་རང་ལ་ཐིམ། ཕར་གཏོང་དུས་བདེ་དགེ་སེམས་ཅན་ལ་ཐིམ་པར་བསམ་མོ། །གཉིས་པ་རྗེས་ཐོབ་ནི།

As for the former, **practice sending and taking alternately.**

Love all living beings as your mother and meditate with potent compassion on the suffering they now experience. Imagine that whatever harms these mothers—all torments of suffering and emotions—enters your heart. Wish fervently for the joy of having this actually happen. What can relieve our mothers' distress? They are helped by happiness and virtue. Therefore, we meditate that as all of our joy and goodness is absorbed by our mothers, they instantly become happy, all conditions for accomplishing Dharma practice are complete, and they are able to attain enlightenment.

**Place these two on the breath.**

Meditate that when you breathe in, the negativities and pain of beings dissolve into you; when you breathe out, your happiness and virtue are absorbed by beings.

As for the latter, post-meditation, there are:

ཡུལ་གསུམ་དུག་གསུམ་དགེ་རྩ་གསུམ། ཞེས་པས་ཡུལ་ཡིད་དུ་འོང་མི་འོང་བར་མ་གསུམ་ལ་བརྟེན་ནས་ཆགས་སྡང་རྨོངས་གསུམ་སྐྱེས་པའི་སེམས་ཅན་མང་པོ་ཡོད་པས་དེ་རྣམས་ཀྱི་དུག་གསུམ་རང་ལ་ཐིམ་ནས་ཆགས་སྡང་གཏི་མུག་མེད་པའི་དགེ་རྩ་གསུམ་དང་ལྡན་པར་གྱུར་ཅིག་སྙམ་དུ་བསམ། སྤྱོད་ལམ་ཀུན་ཏུ་ཚིག་གིས་སྦྱངས། ཞེས་པས་སེམས་ཅན་རྣམས་ཀྱི་སྡིག་པ་དང་སྡུག་བསྔལ་ཐམས་ཅད་བདག་ལ་སྨིན་ཅིང་། བདག་གི་བདེ་བ་དང་དགེ་བ་ཐམས་ཅད་སེམས་ཅན་རྣམས་ལ་སྨིན་པར་གྱུར་ཅིག །ཅེས་ཁ་ཏོན་བྱ། ལེན་པའི་གོ་རིམ་རང་ནས་བརྩམས། ཞེས་པས་རང་ལ་མ་འོངས་པ་ན་འབྱུང་རྒྱུའི་སྡུག་བསྔལ་རྣམས་ད་ལྟ་བླངས་པས་གཞན་སྡུག་ཀྱང་ལེན་ནུས་པར་འགྱུར་རོ། །

**Three objects, three poisons,
three roots of goodness.**

A great many beings develop attachment, aversion, and ignorance because they find objects to be attractive, unappealing, or in between. Therefore, imagine that once their three poisons have dissolved into you, they become endowed with the three roots of goodness free from attachment, aversion, and mental opacity.

**Use bywords to train in every kind of activity.**

Recite aloud: May all sentient beings' negativities and suffering mature in me, and may all of my happiness and goodness ripen in all sentient beings.

**When taking, begin with yourself.**

Through accepting right now all of the suffering that is supposed to be experienced in the future, may I also be able to relieve others of their pain.

གསུམ་པ་རྐྱེན་ངན་བྱང་ཆུབ་ལམ་དུ་བསྒྱུར་བ་ལ། སྣོད་བཅུད་སྡིག་པས་གང་བའི་ཚེ། རྐྱེན་ངན་བྱང་ཆུབ་ལམ་དུ་བསྒྱུར། ཞེས་པས་སྡིག་ལས་ཀྱི་འབྲས་བུ་སྨིན་པས་སྣོད་ཀྱི་འཇིག་རྟེན་གྱི་འབྱོར་པ་ཉམས་བཅུད་ཀྱི་སེམས་ཅན་མ་རུངས་པར་གྱུར་པ་ན། དེ་ལམ་དུ་འཁྱེར་བ་ལ་བསམ་སྦྱོར་གཉིས་ལས་དང་པོ་ལ་ཀུན་རྫོབ་བྱང་སེམས་ཀྱིས་བསྒྱུར་བ་ནི། ལེ་ལན་ཐམས་ཅད་གཅིག་ལ་གདའ། ཞེས་པས་བདག་མེད་ན་སྡུག་བསྔལ་རྒྱུ་ཡང་མེད་པ་ལ། བདག་ཏུ་བཟུང་བས་བདག་གིས་དགྲ་གཉེན་མང་དུ་བྱུང་། དེ་ནས་མཐོ་བ་ལ་ཕྲག་དོག། དམའ་བ་ལ་བརྙས་བཅོས། མཉམ་པ་ལ་འགྲན་སེམས་ཐམས་ཅད་བྱུང་།

·◊· **The third point** is **transforming adverse circumstances into the path** towards enlightenment.

**When the whole world is filled with iniquity,**
**transform adverse circumstances into**
**the path of awakening.**

When the karmic consequences of iniquity ripen, the resources of the outer container—the world—degenerate, and its occupants—sentient beings—misbehave. Integrate this situation into the path through both attitude and deeds.

To transform the first of these, [your attitude,] through conventional bodhicitta:

**Of all that is blameworthy,**
**focus on one thing only.**

If there is no ego, there is no cause for suffering. Once a self is clung to, many friends and enemies appear. All jealousy towards superiors, condescension towards inferiors, and rivalry towards equals have arisen from this.

བདག་གཅེས་འཛིན་དང་སྲིད་འདོད་ཐམས་ཅད་ཀྱང་བྱུང་། དེ་རྣམས་བྱུང་བས་སྡུག་བསྔལ་ཐམས་ཅད་བྱུང་བ་ཡིན་པས་སྡུག་བསྔལ་གྱི་རྩ་བ་བདག་འཛིན་གཅིག་པུར་འདུག །དེ་ནི་བདག་མེད་པ་ལ་ཅིའི་ཕྱིར་བདག་ཏུ་འཛིན་སྙམ་པའི་དྲན་པ་ཡང་ཡང་བསྐྱེད༑ བདག་འཛིན་ནི་སྐྱེས་དུས་དགྲར་བལྟས་ནས་སྤང་ངོ་།།

ཀུན་ལ་བཀའ་དྲིན་ཆེ་བར་བསྒོམ། ཞེས་པས་སངས་རྒྱས་ཐོབ་པ་དེ་ཡང་སེམས་ཅན་ལ་བྱམས་སྙིང་རྗེ་བསྒོམས། སྦྱིན་པ་བཏང་། བཟོད་པ་བསྒོམ་པས་བྱུང་བ་ཡིན། དེས་ན། སེམས་ཅན་མེད་ན་རང་གིས་སངས་རྒྱས་ཀྱང་མི་ཐོབ་པས། རང་ལ་སངས་རྒྱས་དང་སེམས་ཅན་གཉིས་བཀའ་དྲིན་ཁྱད་མེད། ཁྱད་པར་གནོད་སྐྱེལ་མཁན་ཐམས་ཅད། དགེ་བའི་བཤེས་གཉེན་ལྟར་བཀའ་དྲིན་ཆེ་བར་བསྒོམས་ནས། དྲིན་ལན་གཞལ་བའི་ཚུལ་དུ། གནོད་ལན་དུ་ཕན་འདོགས་དངོས་སུ་མ་ནུས་ཀྱང་བསམ་པ་དང་ཚིག་གི་སྒོ་ནས་ཀྱང་ཕན་པ་སྒྲུབ་པོ།།

All self-cherishing and desire for pleasure have arisen from this. Once these have been generated, they then give rise to every form of suffering. Thus, the sole origin of suffering is ego-clinging. Now then, if there is no 'I', why do we reinforce this belief in a self over and over again? When ego-clinging arises, recognize it as the enemy and get rid of it.

### Cultivate deep gratitude towards everyone.

Those who have attained Buddhahood did so by cultivating lovingkindness, compassion, generosity and patience towards living beings. It follows that if there were no sentient beings, we could not attain enlightenment; therefore, for us, there is no difference between the kindness of buddhas and that of sentient beings. Especially, consider that all those who cause harm are as benevolent as spiritual friends. To repay their beneficence, even if unable to respond to injury by tangibly helping them, we bring about their benefit by means of wishes and words.

མདོར་ན་གླང་རི་ཐང་པའི་ཞལ་ནས། ངས་ཇི་ཙམ་གྱི་ཆོས་ཟབ་མོ་ཞིག་ཁ་ཕྱེ་སྟེ་བལྟས་ཀྱང་སྐྱོན་ཐམས་ཅད་རང་གི་ཡིན། ཡོན་ཏན་ཐམས་ཅད་རྗེ་བོ་སེམས་ཅན་གྱི་ཡིན་པར་འདུག ། དེའི་གནད་ཀས། ཁེ་དང་རྒྱལ་ཁ་གཞན་ལ་ཕྱིན། གྱོང་དང་ཕམ་ཁ་རང་གིས་ལེན་པ་འདི་མིན་པ་གོ་རྒྱུ་མེད་གསུངས་པ་ལྟར་ཉམས་སུ་ལེན་དགོས་སོ། །དོན་དམ་བྱང་སེམས་ཀྱིས་རྐྱེན་ངན་ལམ་དུ་བསྒྱུར་བ་ནི། འཁྲུལ་སྣང་སྒྱུ་བཞིན་སྒོམ་པ་ཡི། །སྟོང་ཉིད་སྣང་བ་ཟླ་ན་མེད། ཅེས་གསུངས་པས་སྡུག་བསྔལ་དང་རྐྱེན་ངན་ཐམས་ཅད་རང་སེམས་འཁྲུལ་བས་སྣང་བ་ཡིན། འཁྲུལ་པ་དེ་ཉིད་ཀྱང་ཡེ་ཤེས་ཡིན་ཏེ། སྡུག་བསྔལ་དེའི་ངོ་བོ་ལ་བལྟས་པས་གང་ནས་ཀྱང་མ་སྐྱེས་པས་ཆོས་སྐུ། དེ་ལ་འགག་རྒྱུ་མེད་པས་ལོངས་སྐུ། བར་དུ་གནས་པ་མེད་པས་སྤྲུལ་སྐུ།

In brief, according to Langri Tangpa: "Among all the many profound Dharma teachings I have consulted and perused, 'all faults are mine, all qualities belong to venerable sentient beings' is the key point. Therefore, give profit and victory to others and take loss and defeat upon yourself. Other than this, there's nothing to understand." You should practice according to this maxim.

To transform adverse circumstances into the path through ultimate bodhicitta, as is taught:

**Meditate on appearances arising from confusion as being the four kayas: emptiness is the supreme protection.**

All forms of suffering and undesirable circumstances emerge from the mind's confused projections. Yet the very nature of confusion is wisdom. Observe the essence of suffering. Since it does not arise from anywhere at all, it is dharmakaya, the dimension of absolute reality. Since there is nothing that will cease, it is sambhogakaya, the dimension of perfect enjoyment. Since in between there is nothing that

དེ་རྣམས་དབྱེར་མེད་ངོ་བོ་ཉིད་ཀྱི་སྐུ་ཡིན་པས་སོ། །གཉིས་པ་སྦྱོར་བ་བསག་སྦྱང་གིས་རྒྱུན་ངན་ལམ་དུ་བསྒྱུར་བ་ནི། སྦྱོར་བ་བཞི་ལྡན་ཐབས་ཀྱི་མཆོག །ཅེས་པས་དང་པོ་ཚོགས་བསོག་པའི་སྦྱོར་བ་ནི། རང་བདེ་བ་འདོད་པའི་བློ་སྐྱེས་པའི་ཚེ། བདེ་བ་འདོད་ན་བདེ་བའི་རྒྱུ་ཚོགས་བསག་དགོས་པའི་བརྫ་ཡིན་སླམ་པ་བྲུས་ལ། བླ་མ་དཀོན་མཆོག་མཆོད་པ། དགེ་འདུན་ལ་བསླེན་བཀུར། འབྲུང་པོའི་གཏོར་མ་སོགས་སྒོ་གསུམ་གྱི་སྒོ་ནས་ཚོགས་བསག །བླ་མ་དཀོན་མཆོག་ལ་གསོལ་བ་དྲག་ཏུ་བཏབ་ནས། །བདག་ན་བ་ལེགས་ན་ན་བར་བྱིན་གྱིས་བརླབ་ཏུ་གསོལ། སོས་པ་ལེགས་ན་སོས་པར་བྱིན་གྱིས་བརླབ་ཏུ་གསོལ།

abides, it is nirmanakaya, the dimension of emanation. Since these kayas are indivisible, it is svabhavikakaya, the dimension of the essential nature.

Second, transforming adverse circumstances into the path through accumulation and purification practices:

**The supreme method is comprised of the four activities.**

The first of these is the activity of accumulating merit. Whenever you feel that you would like to be happy, consider that this wish for happiness is a sign that you should accumulate merit, the cause of happiness. Accumulate merit through body, speech, and mind by making offerings to the lama and the three jewels, serving the sangha, offering tormas to elemental spirits, and so on.

Having fervently prayed to the lama and the three jewels, say: "If it is preferable that I be sick, pray grant the blessing of illness; if it preferable that I recover, pray grant the blessing of healing;

ཞི་བ་ལེགས་ན་ཞི་བར་བྱིན་གྱིས་བརླབ་ཏུ་གསོལ། ཞེས་བརྗོད་དོ། །གཉིས་པ་སྡིག་པ་སྦྱང་བའི་སྦྱོར་བ་ནི། རང་སྡུག་བསྔལ་སྤྱོད་པའི་བློ་སྐྱེས་པའི་ཚེ། དེའི་རྒྱུ་སྡིག་པ་སྤྱོད་དགོས་པའི་བརྡ་ཡིན་སྙམ་པ་བྱས་ལ། སྔར་བྱས་ལ་འགྱོད་པས་བཤགས་པ་དང་། ཕྱིན་ཆད་མི་བྱ་བའི་སྡོམ་སེམས་དང་། སྡིག་པ་སྦྱང་བའི་ཐབས་ལ་སྒོ་དུ་མ་ནས་འབད་དོ། །གསུམ་པ་གདོན་ལ་མཆོད་པ་ནི། གདོན་བགེགས་ཀྱི་བར་ཆད་བྱུང་བའི་ཚེ་གཏོར་མ་ཕུལ་ལ་བཀའ་དྲིན་ཆེ་བར་བལྟ་བའམ། དེ་ཙམ་མི་ནུས་ཀྱང་གཏོར་མ་བྱིན་ལ། ངའི་ཆོས་ཀྱི་བར་ཆད་མ་བྱེད། ངས་ཁྱོད་གང་ཕན་པ་དེ་སྒྲུབ་བོ་ཞེས་བརྗོད་དོ། །བཞི་པ་ཆོས་སྐྱོང་ལ་མཆོད་པ་ནི། གཏོར་མ་ཕུལ་ལ། ཆོས་སྒྲུབ་པའི་འགལ་རྐྱེན་ཞི་བ་དང་མཐུན་རྐྱེན་འགྲུབ་པར་གསོལ་བ་གདབ་བོ། །

if it is preferable that I die, pray grant the blessing of death."

The second is the activity of purifying negativities. Whenever you feel that you would like to be free from suffering, consider that this is a sign that you should abandon the cause of suffering: misdeeds. Confess those of the past with remorse, resolve not to commit others in the future, and strive to forsake negative actions through the many available methods.

The third is making offerings to malevolent forces. Whenever obstacles arise due to malevolent and obstructing forces, offer them [the ritual dough objects called] tormas with a deeply grateful frame of mind. Otherwise, if this much is impossible, as you offer tormas say: "Do not create obstacles to my Dharma practice. I will do whatever I can to help you."

The fourth is making offerings to the Dharma protectors. As you offer them tormas, pray that all circumstances which hinder Dharma practice are pacified and favorable conditions are established.

འཕྲལ་ལ་གང་ཐུག་བསྒོམ་དུ་སྒྱུར། ཞེས་པས་རང་ལ་ནད་གདོན་དགྲ་ལ་སོགས་པའི་སྡུག་བསྔལ་གློ་བུར་འཕྲལ་དུ་བྱུང་ན་འཇིག་རྟེན་གྱི་ཁམས་ན་འདི་ལྟར་སྡུག་བསྔལ་ཆེ་བ་དཔག་མེད་ཡོད་པ་དེ་ཐམས་ཅད་བདག་ལ་འདུས་པར་གྱུར་ཅིག་སྙམ་དུ་ཞེ་ཐག་པ་ནས་བསམ་མོ། །

**Join unexpected events with your practice.**

If unexpected tribulations such as illness, negative forces, enemies and so forth befall you all of a sudden, think with the utmost sincerity: "In our universe, there is no end to the different kinds of intense suffering similar to this. May they all gather into myself."

བཞི་པ་ཚེ་གཅིག་གི་ཉམས་ལེན་དྲིལ་ནས་བསྟན་པ་ནི། མན་ངག་སྙིང་པོ་མདོར་བསྡུས་པ། །སྟོབས་ལྔ་དག་དང་སྦྱར་བར་བྱ། ཞེས་པས་དང་པོ་འཕེན་པའི་སྟོབས་ནི། ད་ནས་བཟུང་སྟེ་ཟླ་བ་འདི་དང་ལོ་འདི་དང་མ་ཤིའི་བར་དང་། སངས་མ་རྒྱས་ཀྱི་བར་དུ་བྱང་ཆུབ་ཀྱི་སེམས་གཉིས་དང་མི་བྲལ་བར་བྱའོ། །ཞེས་བློའི་འཕེན་པ་དྲག་པོ་བྱའོ། །གཉིས་པ་གོམས་པའི་སྟོབས་ནི། ཡང་དང་ཡང་དུ་བྱང་ཆུབ་སེམས་གཉིས་སྦྱོང་བའོ། །གསུམ་པ་དཀར་པོ་ས་བོན་གྱི་སྟོབས་ནི། བྱང་ཆུབ་ཀྱི་སེམས་སྐྱེ་བ་དང་འཕེལ་བའི་དོན་དུ་ཅི་ནུས་ཀྱི་ཚོགས་བསག་པའོ། །བཞི་པ་སུན་འབྱིན་པའི་སྟོབས་ནི། བདག་གཅེས་འཛིན་གྱི་བློ་སྐྱེས་ན་སྔར་ཡང་འདིས་སྡུག་བསྔལ་ལ་སྦྱར། ཚེ་འདིར་ཡང་ཆོས་མི་ཡོང་བ་དེ་འདིས་ལན་སླམ་པ་བྱས་ལ་རྒྱངས་ཀྱིས་སྤང་བར་བྱའོ། །

◈ **The fourth point** shows how to **incorporate the practice in one's lifetime.**

**The epitome of the pith instructions**
**is the application of the five powers.**

The first is the compelling power. Compel your mind forcefully thus: "From now on—this month, this year, until I die, until I have reached Buddhahood—I will never be separated from the two aspects of awakening mind."

The second is the power of familiarization. Train again and again in both [ultimate and relative] bodhicittas.

The third is the power of sowing white seeds. Accumulate merit by doing everything you can to generate and enhance awakening mind.

The fourth is the power of disenchantment. When self-cherishing arises, respond with the thought: "In the past, I have met with suffering because of this, and in this life too it precludes the [practice of] Dharma," and do away with it.

ལྟ་བ་སྨོན་ལམ་གྱི་སྟོབས་ནི། དགེ་སྦྱོར་ཐམས་ཅད་ཀྱི་
གཞིམ་དུ། བྱང་ཆུབ་སེམས་དང་མི་འབྲལ་ཞིང་། །བྱང་
ཆུབ་སྤྱོད་ལ་གཞོལ་བ་དང་། །སངས་རྒྱས་རྣམས་ཀྱིས་
ཡོངས་བཟུང་ནས། །བདུད་ཀྱི་ལས་རྣམས་སྤོང་བར་ཤོག།
ཅེས་སྨོན་ལམ་གདབ། དེ་བཞིན་འབྱུང་བར་བླ་མ་དཀོན་
མཆོག་ལ་གསོལ་བ་གདབ་བོ། །ཐེག་ཆེན་འཕོ་བའི་གདམས་
ངག་ནི། །སྟོབས་ལྔ་ཉིད་ཡིན་སྤྱོད་ལམ་གཅེས། ཅེས་
པས་དཀར་པོ་ས་བོན་གྱི་སྟོབས་སུ་ཡོ་བྱད་ཡོད་ཚད་མཆོད་སྦྱིན་
དུ་བཏང་། སྨོན་ལམ་གྱི་སྟོབས་སུ་བླ་མ་དཀོན་མཆོག་ལ་
གསོལ་བ་བཏབ། བྱང་སེམས་འབྱོངས་པའི་སྨོན་ལམ་
གདབ་བོ། །སུན་འབྱིན་པའི་སྟོབས་སུ་ད་ལྟ་ཡང་ལུས་འདི་
ལ་བདག་ཏུ་གཅེས་པར་བཟུང་བས་སྡུག་བསྔལ་བར་འདུག །
བརྟགས་ན་བདག་ནི་གང་དུ་ཡང་མི་འདུག་སྙམ་པ་བྱས་ལ་
བདག་འཛིན་སྤང་ངེས།

The fifth is the power of aspirations. Following all virtuous practices, recite this aspiration prayer: "May I never be separated from awakening mind and may I apply myself wholeheartedly to enlightened activities. Now that the buddhas have taken me in their care, may the maras' actions be dispelled." Pray to the lama and the three jewels that this will happen as expressed.

**The Mahayana instructions for dying are the same five powers. Conduct is essential.**

For the power of sowing white seeds, give away everything you own as offerings and donations.

For the power of aspirations, pray to the lama and three jewels and formulate the wish to perfectly accomplish bodhicitta.

For the power of disenchantment, think: "Even now I have been suffering because of clinging to the idea of a cherished self in this body. But when examined, there is nothing whatsoever which is a 'self'." With this, self-clinging will surely cease.

འཕེན་པའི་སྟོབས་སུ་ངས་བར་དོ་དང་སྐྱེ་བ་ཕྱི་མར་ཡང་བྱང་ཆུབ་
ཀྱི་སེམས་སྦྱང་བར་བྱ་སྙམ་པ་བསམ། གོམས་པའི་སྟོབས་
སུ་དང་པོར་ཀུན་རྫོབ་བྱང་སེམས་ཀྱི་གཏོང་ལེན་རླུང་ལ་བསྐྱོན་
ནས་སྦྱང་། དེ་ནས་བློས་ཅིར་ཡང་མི་འཛིན་དོན་དམ་བྱང་
སེམས་ཀྱི་ངང་ལ་མཉམ་པར་བཞག་གོ །སྤྱོད་ལམ་ནི་
གཞོགས་གཡས་འོག་ཏུ་བཅུག །ལག་པ་གཡས་པས་
འགྲམ་པ་བརྟེན་ཏེ་མཐེའུ་ཆུང་གིས་སྣ་བུག་གཡས་བཀག་ལ་
རླུང་གཡོན་ནས་རྒྱུ་བར་བྱའོ། །རྫས་ཀྱི་རྟེན་འབྲེལ་དུ།
རྡོ་ཁབ་ལེན་དང་འགྲོན་བུའི་ཕྱེ་མ་བསྲེགས་པ་ཞིབ་ཏུ་བཏགས་ལ་
སྦྲང་སྦྱོན་གྱིས་བྲུས་པ་རིལ་བུ་སྲན་མ་ཙམ་བྱས། འཆི་ལ་
ཐུག་པ་དང་དེ་ཆང་སྦྱར་ནས་སྤྱི་གཙུག་ཏུ་བྱུག་གོ །

For the compelling power, think: "I will train in awakening mind during the bardo and the next lives."

As for the power of familiarization, begin with purification via the relative bodhicitta practice of tonglen that rides the breath. Then, settle within the meditative equipoise of ultimate bodhicitta free from any conceptual grasping.

Conduct entails lying on the right side of the body with your right hand supporting your cheek. Block the right nostril with your little finger, so that your breath comes and goes from the left nostril. As for propitious substances, thoroughly grind a powder of magnetite and burnt cowry shells, mix it with wild honey, and make pea-sized pills beforehand. When the moment of death is nigh, mix them with ale and rub some on the crown of the head.

ལྔ་པ་བློ་འབྱོངས་པའི་ཚད་བསྟན་པ་ནི། ཆོས་ཀུན་དགོངས་པ་གཅིག་ཏུ་འདུས། ཞེས་པས་ཐེག་པ་ཆེ་ཆུང་གི་ཆོས་ཐམས་ཅད་ཀྱི་དགོས་པ་བདག་འཛིན་འདུལ་བར་འདུས། བདག་གི་གཉེན་པོར་མ་སོང་འདུག་ན་ཆོས་བྱས་ཚད་དོན་མེད་དུ་སོང་བ་ཡིན། དེའི་གཉེན་པོར་སོང་འདུག་པ་བློ་སྦྱོང་རྒྱུད་ལ་སྐྱེས་པ་ཡིན་ནོ། །དཔང་པོ་གཉིས་ཀྱི་གཙོ་བོ་བཟུང་། ཞེས་པས་ཕྱི་མདོག་ནས་མི་གཞན་གྱིས་ཆོས་པར་མཐོང་ཞིང་གྲུས་པ་ཡང་དཔང་པོ་ཡིན་མོད། དེ་ནི་གཙོ་བོར་མི་བཟུང་སྟེ། མི་ཐལ་གྱིས་བདག་གི་སེམས་མི་རྟོག །སྤྱོད་ལམ་ལེགས་པ་རེ་མཐོང་ན་མགུ་སྤྲིད་པས་སོ། །དིས་ན་རང་གི་རང་ལ་མ་ཁྲེལ་བ་དེ་གཙོ་བོར་བཟུང་ངོ་། །

⟡ **The fifth point** presents how to **evaluate progress in mind training.**

**All Dharma is united in one objective.**

In Mahayana and Hinayana traditions alike, the objective of all forms of the Dharma involves subduing ego-clinging. If Dharma has not been effective as an antidote to ego, then our entire practice has been useless. If it has been effective as an antidote, then lojong–mind training–has truly dawned within us.

**Of two witnesses, heed the more important one.**

If your general appearance is such that others see you as a practitioner and respect you, it is indeed a testimony, but not the most important one. Ordinary people cannot read your thoughts; if they happen to catch you engaging in positive conduct, they may be quite impressed. But *you* know if you have nothing to be ashamed of; therefore, the most important witness is you.

ཡིད་བདེ་འབབ་ཞིག་རྒྱུན་དུ་བསྟེན། །ཞེས་པས་ད་ཕྱིན་ཆད་རྐྱེན་ངན་ཅི་བྱུང་ཡང་བློ་སྦྱོང་གིས་ལམ་དུ་ཁྱེར་བས་ཚོག་སྙམ་དུ་ཉམ་ང་མེད་པས་བདེ་བར་བྱའོ། །ཡིངས་ཀྱང་ཐུབ་ན་འབྱོངས་པ་ཡིན། ཞེས་པས་རྟ་རྩལ་ཅན་ཡིངས་ཀྱང་རྟ་ལས་མི་ལྷུང་བ་ལྟར། གློ་བུར་དུ་གནོད་བྱེད་སོགས་བྱུང་ཀྱང་ཞེ་སྡང་མི་སྐྱེ་བར་བློ་སྦྱོང་གི་གྲོགས་སུ་འགྲོ་འདུག་ན་བློ་འབྱོངས་པ་ཡིན་ནོ། །འབྱོངས་པའི་ཚད་འདི་དག་ནི་བློ་སྦྱོང་རྒྱུད་ལ་སྐྱེས་པའི་རྟགས་ཡིན་གྱི། འབྱོངས་ཟེར་ནས་ད་སྦྱང་མི་དགོས་པ་ནི་མ་ཡིན་ཏེ། སངས་རྒྱས་མ་ཐོབ་པར་སྦྱང་དགོས་སོ། །

**An ever-serene mind is the only recourse.**

From now on, even if a calamitous situation were to arise, it would be acceptable because you could incorporate it into the path of mind training. With this thought, nothing poses a threat, so relax.

**If you are able even when distracted, you have trained well.**

Even when distracted, able riders do not fall from their horses. Similarly, even when harm-doers and their like suddenly appear, if we do not experience anger but use [the situation] to enhance our lojong practice, the mind has been well-trained.

These evaluations of training show whether lojong has developed in your mind, but that does not mean that when one has "trained well," one need train no longer. Training must continue until Buddhahood has been achieved!

དུག་པ་བློ་སྦྱོང་གི་དམ་ཚིག་བསྟན་པ་ནི། སྤྱི་དོན་གསུམ་ལ་

རྟག་ཏུ་བསླབ། ཅེས་པས་སྤྱི་དོན་དང་པོ་ཁས་བླངས་དང་མི་

འགལ་བ་ནི། བློ་སྦྱོང་བ་ཡིན་ཟེར་ནས་བསླབ་པ་ཕྲ་མོ་ཁྱད་དུ་

གསོད་པ་མི་བྱ་བར། སོ་ཐར་ནས་རྡོ་རྗེ་ཐེག་པའི་བར།

རང་གིས་ཇི་ལྟར་ཁས་བླངས་པའི་བསླབ་པ་རྣམས་མ་ཉམས་པར་

བསྲུང་བར་བྱའོ། །སྤྱི་དོན་གཉིས་པ་ཐོ་ཅོར་མ་ཤོར་བ་ནི།

བདག་གཅེས་འཛིན་ཡོད་པ་གཞན་གྱིས་གོ་བར་བྱ་བའི་ཕྱིར་ཤིང་

གཉན་པོ་གཅོད་པ་དང་། མཚོ་ཕོ་དང་འགྲོགས་པ་སོགས་ཐོ་

ཅོའི་སྤྱོད་པ་རྣམས་སྤང་ངོ་། །སྤྱི་དོན་གསུམ་པ་ཕྱོགས་རེར་

མ་ལྷུང་བ་ནི། མིའི་གནོད་པ་བཟོད་ལ་ལྷ་འདྲེའི་གནོད་པ་མི་

བཟོད་པ་དང་། ཆེ་བ་ལ་གུས་ལ་ཆུང་བ་ལ་བརྙས་པ་དང་།

གཉེན་ལ་བྱམས་ལ་དགྲ་ལ་སྡང་བ་ལ་སོགས་ཕྱོགས་རེ་བ

ཐམས་ཅད་སྤངས་ལ་སྙོམས་པར་སྤྱང་ངོ་། །

⟡ **The sixth point** presents the lojong precepts.

**Always train in the three basic principles.**

The first basic principle concerns not transgressing your commitments. If you call yourself a lojong practitioner, you must not brush aside even minor precepts. From individual liberation vows to those of vajrayana, however many precepts you have committed yourself to should be maintained faultlessly.

The second basic principle concerns refraining from nonsensical behavior. All reckless acts—such as cutting down haunted trees or keeping company with lepers in order to convince others that you are free of self-cherishing—should be abandoned.

The third basic principle concerns not falling into partial behavior. Train in equanimity by rejecting all forms of partiality, such as being patient when people aggress you but not when gods or demons do; respecting those who are important and scorning those who are not; being kind to loved ones and hostile to enemies, and so on.

འདུན་པ་བསྒྱུར་བ་རང་སོར་བཞག །ཅེས་པ་སྟར་བདག
གཅེས་པར་འཛིན་པ་དེ། ད་གཞན་གཅེས་འཛིན་དུ་བསྒྱུར་ལ་
ལུས་ངག་གི་སྤྱོད་པ་ཆོས་མཐུན་རང་སོ་ཐུབ་པར་བྱ། བློ་སྤྱོང་
ཐམས་ཅད་མདོན་ཚན་ཆུང་ལ་ཆོད་ཆེ་བ་ཅིག་བྱེད་དགོས་
གསུངས་པས། གཞན་གྱིས་མ་ཆོར་བར་རང་རྒྱུད་སྨིན་ཟིན་
པ་ཞིག་བྱའོ། །ཡན་ལག་ཉམས་པ་བརྗོད་མི་བྱ། ཞེས་
པས་གཞན་ལ་འཛིག་རྟེན་གྱི་སྐྱོན་ཡོད་བ་སོགས་དང་། ཆོས་
ཀྱི་སྐྱོན་གཞན་ཚུལ་ཁྲིམས་འཆལ་བ་སོགས་མི་སྙན་པའི་ཚིག་
རྣམས་མི་བརྗོད་དོ། །གཞན་ཕྱོགས་གང་ཡང་མི་བསམ་མོ།།
ཞེས་པས་སྐྱིར་སེམས་ཅན་ཐམས་ཅད་དང་། ཁྱད་པར་ཆོས་
སྒོར་ཞུགས་པ་རྣམས་ལ་སྐྱོན་མཐོང་ན། ང་རང་སྣང་བ་མ་
དག་པ་ཡིན།

## Transform your approach while remaining natural.

You used to treasure yourself above all. Now that others have become more important, your physical behavior should be consistent with Dharma while remaining natural. It is said that lojong practice must be very effective yet very discreet; it should ripen in your mindstream without being obvious to others.

## Do not speak of others' infirmities.

Do not use harsh words to speak of others' physical impairments, such as blindness, or Dharma-related failings, such as unseemly moral conduct.

## Never judge others.

If you see others' faults, those of living beings in general and more specifically those of people who have entered the gates of the Dharma,

ཁོང་ལ་དེ་འདྲའི་སྐྱོན་ཉེན་མེད་སྙམ་དུ་བསམ་མོ། །ཉོན་
མོངས་གང་ཆེ་སྟོན་ལ་སྦྱང་། ཞེས་པས་རང་རྒྱུད་ལ་ཉོན་
མོངས་གང་ཆེ་བརྟགས་ནས། གང་ཆེ་བ་དེའི་གཉེན་པོར་
ཐམས་ཅད་སྤངས་ནས་དེ་ཉིད་ཐོག་མར་འདུལ་ལོ། །འབྲས་
བུར་རེ་བ་ཐམས་ཅད་སྤངས། ཞེས་པས་བློ་སྦྱོང་བྱས་པས་ཚེ་
འདིའི་རྙེད་བཀུར་ལ་སོགས་པ་དང་། ཕྱི་མ་ལྷ་མིའི་བདེ་བ་
དང་། རང་ཉིད་ཁོ་ན་མྱང་འདས་ཐོབ་པར་འདོད་པ་སོགས་
རང་དོན་ཐམས་ཅད་སྤང་པར་བྱའོ། །དུག་ཅན་གྱི་ཟས་སྤང་།
ཞེས་པས་དངོས་པོ་བདེན་འཛིན་དང་བདག་གཅིས་འཛིན་དང་
འབྲེས་པའི་དགེ་སྦྱོར་ཐམས་ཅད་ཟས་དུག་དང་འབྲེས་པ་དང་འདྲ་
བས་དེ་སྤོང་བའོ། །

think: "This must be my own impure perception—they cannot possibly have such faults."

**Purify whichever affliction is the strongest first.**

Once you have identified which of your emotional afflictions is the strongest, gather together all of its antidotes and subdue that affliction first.

**Abandon all hope of results.**

As you practice lojong, you should abandon all self-centered desires such as wishing for wealth and honor in this life, the happiness of gods or humans in the next, or wanting to attain nirvana for yourself alone.

**Avoid poisoned food.**

Mixing any virtuous practice with the assumption that things actually exist and self-cherishing is like mixing food with poison, so give it up.

གཞུང་བཟང་པོ་མ་བསྟེན། ཞེས་པ་ཞི་ནག་མི་བྱེད་པའོ།།

ཤགས་ངན་མ་རྒོད། ཅེས་པས་གཞན་གྱི་ཚིག་ངན་ལ་ལན་དུ་ཚིག་ངན་སྨྲ་བ་དང་། གཞན་གྱི་ཉེས་པ་ལ་གྲོང་ཁ་བདའ་བ་སོགས་མི་བྱའོ། །འཕྲང་མ་སྒྲུགས། ཅེས་པས་གཞན་གྱིས་གནོད་པ་བྱས་པ་ཞི་ལ་བཞག་ནས་གནོད་ལན་འཁྱོལ་དུས་བྱུང་ན་སྐྱིལ་བ་དེ་སྤང་ངོ་། །གནད་ལ་མི་དབབ། ཅེས་པས་མིའི་སྐྱོན་མཚང་ནས་འབྲུ་བ་དང་། མི་མ་ཡིན་གྱི་སྲོག་སྔགས་བཟླ་བ་སོགས་གཞན་སེམས་ལ་གནོད་པ་དྲག་པོ་འབྱུང་བ་མི་བྱེད་དོ། །

**Do not make a point of constancy.**

Do not harbor resentment.

**Avoid the agitation of hurtful talk.**

Do not answer others' insults with harsh repartees. Do not uncaringly call attention to others' transgressions.

**Do not wait in ambush.**

When others have hurt you, you might keep it hidden in your heart until the time for revenge is nigh. Give it up.

**Do not focus on others' sore points.**

Do not expose people's hidden faults. Nor should you misuse the life-mantras of non-humans or use other methods which may cause great damage to others' minds.

མཛོ་ཁལ་གླང་ལ་མི་འགྲོ། ཞེས་པས་རང་ལ་བབ་པའི་བཅུ་གལ་ལམ་ཁག་ངན། གཡོ་སྒྱུས་གཞན་ལ་སྐྱུར་བའི་ཁོང་སྐྱོན་ཅན་གྱི་སྤྱོད་པ་མི་བྱའོ། །མགྲོགས་ཀྱི་རྩེ་མི་བརྗོད། ཅེས་པས་ལོངས་སྤྱོད་ཐུན་མོང་བ་ཐབས་སླ་ཚོགས་ཀྱིས་རང་ཁོ་ནས་ཐོབ་པ་དེ་འདྲ་མི་བྱའོ། །ལྷོ་ལོག་མི་བྱ། ཞེས་པས་རང་བཟང་པོར་འདོད་ནས་ཕམ་ཁ་ལེན་པ་དང་། འདྲེ་གདོན་ནད་ཞི་བའི་ཕྱིར་གློ་སྟོང་བྱེད་པ་སོགས་ལྷོ་བཅོས་ལྷ་བུ་མི་བྱ། ལྷ་བདུད་དུ་མི་དབབ། ཅེས་པས་གློ་སྟོང་བྱས་པས་ང་རྒྱལ་དང་རློམ་སེམས་ཆེ་རུ་སོང་ན། ཆོས་གནད་དུ་མ་སོང་བར་ཆོས་མིན་དུ་སོང་།

**Do not burden a cow with an ox's load.**

When saddled with an unwelcome duty or reprimand, do not try to cheat and pass it on to others so that they become the patsy.

**Do not play to win.**

Do not use different techniques to acquire collective resources for your private enjoyment.

**Do not misuse magic.**

Do not try to bolster your self-image by taking defeat upon yourself or practicing lojong like a magic ceremony in order to pacify demons, malevolent forces, or maladies.

**Do not turn a god into a demon.**

If the practice of lojong has reinforced your pride and arrogance, then the practice has not been effective, and is Dharma no longer.

འདྲི་ཤར་ནས་གནོད་པ་ལ་གླུད་ནུབ་ཏུ་སྐྱེལ་བ་དང་འདྲ་བས་ཕན་མེད། དེས་ན་བདག་བཟང་འདོད་དང་གཅེས་འཛིན་སྤངས་ལ་ཀུན་ལ་བྲན་གྱི་ཐ་མ་ལྟར་བྱའོ། །སྐྱིད་གྱི་ཡན་ལག་ཏུ་སྡུག་མ་ཚོལ། ཞེས་པས་རང་གི་ཉེ་དུ་དང་གྲོགས་མཆེད་ལ་སོགས་པ་ཤི་ན། དེ་དག་གི་ཟས་ནོར་དང་དཔེ་ཆ་རྟེན་མཆོད་ང་ལ་ཡོང་། ཡོན་བདག་ལ་ན་ཚ་ཤི་ཆད་བྱུང་ན་ང་ལ་ཚོགས་བསོག་ཡོང་། རང་དང་མཉམ་པའི་སྒོམ་ཆེན་ཤི་ན་ང་གཅིག་པུ་ལ་སྐུ་བསོད་ཡོང་། དགྲ་ཤི་ན་གནོད་བྱེད་མི་ཡོང་བས་ང་འཚོངས་སླམ་པ་ལྟ་བུར་སྐྱིད་པའི་ཐབས་སུ་གཞན་སྡུག་པར་འདོད་པ་སྤང་ངོ། །

It is as senseless as trying to placate an evil spirit of the east by sending compensation to the west. Accordingly, having abandoned vanity and self-cherishing, be everyone's most humble servant.

**Do not look to make pain part of pleasure.**

"If my friends or Dharma brethren were to die, their food, money, texts and shrine objects would be mine. If my benefactor were struck by a fatal illness, I would receive plenty of offerings. If a great meditator of my league were to die, his wealth and influence would become mine alone. If my enemy were to die no one would bother me and that would make me happy..." Thoughts such as these—the desire that others might suffer so as to ensure your own pleasure—must be rejected.

བདུན་པ་བློ་སྦྱོང་གི་བསླབ་བྱ་བསྟན་པ་ནི། རྣལ་འབྱོར་ཐམས་ཅད་གཅིག་གིས་བྱ། ཞེས་པ་ཟས་གོས་ཀྱི་རྣལ་འབྱོར་ལ་སོགས་པ་ཐམས་ཅད་ཀྱང་གཞན་ཕན་འབའ་ཞིག་གིས་བྱེད་པའོ།།

ལོག་ནོན་ཐམས་ཅད་གཅིག་གིས་བྱ། ཞེས་པས་བློ་སྦྱོང་བསྒོམས་པས་ན་ཚ་འདྲི་གདོན། མི་རྣམས་སྨད་བ་སོགས་བྱུང་ནས་བློ་སྦྱོང་སྙིང་མི་འདོད་ན། འདི་ལྟ་བུའི་སེམས་ཅན་ཡང་དུ་ཡོད་པས་དེ་དག་གིས་ཉེས་པ་རང་ལ་ཐིམ་པར་གྱུར་ཅིག་སྙམ་དུ་བསམ། ཐོག་མཐའ་གཉིས་ལ་བྱ་བ་གཉིས།

ཞེས་པས་སྔ་དྲོའི་ཐོག་མར་དེའི་རིང་བྱང་ཆུབ་སེམས་གཉིས་དང་མི་འབྲལ་བར་བྱ་དགོས་སྙམ་དུ་འཛིན་པ་བཏང་། དགོང་མོ་ཉལ་ཁར།

⟡ **The seventh point** presents **mind training guidelines.**

**There is one way to do all practices.**

Everything you do, including practices involving food, clothing, and so on, should benefit others.

**Confront all problems with one solution.**

When faced with illness, demons, evil spirits, and people's hatred, if you do not genuinely wish to apply mind training to the situation even though you have been practicing lojong, think: "Most living beings are in the same boat. May their faults dissolve into me."

**In the beginning, in the end: two things to do.**

At the start of the morning, think with great determination: "Today I shall not be separated from the two bodhicittas." In the evening as you go to sleep, consider the day's activities and make

ཉིན་པར་གྱི་སྤྱོད་པ་རྣམས་ལ་བརྟགས་ཏེ། བྱང་ཆུབ་སེམས་དང་འགལ་བ་བྱུང་བ་རང་ལ་མདན་བགྲང་། བཤགས་པ་བྱས་ལ་ཕྱིས་མི་འབྱུང་བར་བྱ། གཉིས་པོ་གང་བྱུང་བཟོད་པར་བྱ། ཞེས་པས་འཁོར་ལོངས་སྤྱོད་མངའ་ཐང་ཕུན་ཚོགས་བྱུང་ཀྱང་དེས་མ་དྲེགས་པར་སྒྱུ་མ་ལྟ་བུར་བསམ། ཤིན་ཏུ་རྒུད་ནས་འོག་ཏུ་འགྲོ་བ་ཆུ་ལས་མེད་པ་བྱུང་ཀྱང་སྒྱུ་མ་ལྟ་བུར་བསམ་ནས་གཏོང་ལེན་སྦྱོང་ཞིང་། ཁེངས་པ་དང་ཞུམ་པ་གང་ཡང་མི་བྱའོ། །གཉིས་པོ་སྲོག་དང་བསྡོམས་ནས་བསྲུང་། ཞེས་པས་ཆོས་སྤྱིའི་དམ་ཚིག་དང་ཁྱད་པར་བློ་སྦྱོང་གི་དམ་ཚིག་གཉིས་སྲོག་དང་འདྲ་བར་བསྲུང་བའོ། །དཀའ་བ་གསུམ་ལ་བསླབ་པར་བྱ། ཞེས་པས་ཉོན་མོངས་པ་སྐྱེས་པ་ན་དང་པོར་དྲན་པར་དཀའ། བར་དུ་བཟློག་པར་དཀའ།

a list of all misdoings that went against bodhicitta. Acknowledge them and make sure they will not happen again.

**Patiently accept whichever of the two occurs.**

Even if you have wealth, power, attendants, and prosperity, do not be proud, but recognize them as an illusion. And even if everything falls apart and you have sunk so low that water is all you have left, think of it as an illusion and practice tonglen. Be neither arrogant nor despondent.

**Keep both as if your life depended on it.**

Guard both the general Dharma precepts and the specific lojong vows as you guard your life.

**Train in the three challenges.**

When negative emotions arise, the first challenge is to be aware of them, the next is to keep them at bay, and the last is to finish them off.

ཐ་མར་རྒྱུན་ཆོད་དཀའ་བས་དང་པོ་ནམ་སྐྱེས་དུས་ངོས་ཟིན་པར་བྱ། བར་དུ་གཉེན་པོས་སྐྱང་། མཐར་ཕྱིས་མི་འབྱུང་བའི་ཐབས་ལ་འབད་པར་བྱའོ། །རྒྱུ་ཡི་གཙོ་བོ་རྣམས་གསུམ་བླང་། ཞེས་པས་བླ་མ་བཟང་པོ་མཛལ་བ་རང་བློ་ལས་སུ་རུང་བས་ཆོས་སྒྲུབ་པ་ཆོས་སྒྲུབ་པའི་མཐུན་རྐྱེན་འཛོམ་པ་གསུམ་བླང་ངོ་།། ཉམས་པ་མེད་པ་རྣམས་གསུམ་བསྒོམ། ཞེས་པས་མོས་གུས་དང་། བློ་སྦྱོང་དང་། ཚུལ་ཁྲིམས་ཀྱི་བསླབ་པ་ཕྲ་མོ་ཚུན་ཆད་མི་ཉམས་པར་བསྲུང་བའོ། །འབྲལ་མེད་གསུམ་དང་ལྡན་པར་བྱ། ཞེས་པས་སྒོ་གསུམ་དགེ་བ་དང་མི་འབྲལ་བར་བྱའོ། །

As for the first, recognize them as soon as they surface. Next, use remedies to dispose of them. Finally, apply whichever methods will keep them from arising in the future.

**Adopt the three principal causes.**

Adopt these three: meeting with an excellent lama, practicing the Dharma with a compliant mind, and gathering appropriate conditions for practice.

**Unfailingly cultivate three things.**

Unfailingly observe devotion, mind training and the rules of moral conduct, including the most minor ones.

**Make sure you have the inseparable three.**

Never separate the body, speech, and mind from virtue.

ཡུལ་ལ་ཕྱོགས་མེད་དག་ཏུ་སྦྱང་། ཁྱབ་དང་གཏིང་འབྱོངས་ཀུན་ལ་གཅེས། ཞེས་པས་སེམས་ཅན་ཐམས་ཅད་ལ་ཁྱབ་པར་བྱས་ལ་ཁ་ཚིག་ཙམ་མིན་པར་ཞེ་ནས་འབྱོངས་པར་བྱའོ།།

བཀོལ་བ་རྣམས་ལ་རྟག་ཏུ་བསྒོམ། ཞེས་པས་རང་དང་ལྷན་ཅིག་འགྲོགས་པ་དང་། རང་དང་འགྲན་ཟླ་དང་། ཕར་གནོད་པ་མ་བྱས་ཀྱང་ཚུར་གནོད་པ་བྱེད་པ་དང་། ལས་དབང་གིས་སྙིང་དུ་མི་སྡུག་པ་སོགས་སྐྱེ་དཀའ་བ་ལ་ལྷག་པར་བསྒོམ་པའོ། །རྐྱེན་གཞན་དག་ལ་ལྟོས་མི་བྱ། ཞེས་པས་ཟས་གོས་འཚོམ་མ་འཚོམ། གནོད་པ་ཡོད་མེད། གནས་སྐྱིད་སྡུག་ཁམས་བཟང་ངན་སོགས་ལ་མི་ལྟོས་པར་བྱའོ། །

**Train impartially in every instance. Once deep and inclusive training has taken place, love everyone.**

Train wholeheartedly, not just rhetorically. Encompass all living beings in your training.

**Always practice with special cases.**

Your companions and rivals; those far removed who have not harmed you and those close by who have; those whom you instinctively dislike because of karma, and so on: make these difficult cases the special object of your practice.

**Do not concern yourself with external circumstances.**

Do not concern yourself with whether or not there is an abundance of food and clothing; whether or not there is suffering; whether your lodgings are pleasant or unpleasant; whether your health is good or bad, and so forth.

ད་རེས་གཙོ་བོ་ཉམས་སུ་བླང་། ཞེས་པས་སྔར་ཕན་འཁོར་བར་སྐྱེ་བ་བླངས་པ་ཐམས་ཅད་དོན་མེད་དུ་སོང་། ད་རེས་དོན་གྱི་གཙོ་བོ་ཅིག་སྒྲུབ་དགོས། དེ་ལ། ཚེ་འདིའི་དོན་ལས་ཆོས་གཙོ། བཤད་པ་ལས་སྒྲུབ་པ་གཙོ། སྒྲུབ་པ་གཞན་ལས་བྱང་ཆུབ་ཀྱི་སེམས་གཙོ་བས་དེ་བཞིན་ཉམས་སུ་ལེན་པའོ། །གོ་ལོག་མི་བྱ། ཞེས་པས་ཆོས་ཀྱི་སྡུག་བསྔལ་མི་བཟོད་པར་འཇིག་རྟེན་གྱི་སྡུག་བསྔལ་བཟོད་པར་བཟོད་པ་གོ་ལོག །ཆོས་ལ་མི་འདུན་པར་ཚེ་འདིའི་བྱ་བ་ལ་འདུན་པ་འདུན་པ་གོ་ལོག །ཆོས་ཀྱི་རོ་མི་མྱང་བར་འཇིག་རྟེན་གྱི་རོ་མྱང་བ་རོ་མྱོང་གོ་ལོག །

**Put the most important things into practice now.**

Thus far, taking rebirth in samsara has been senseless; the time has come to accomplish the most important things. These are the Dharma, which is more important than any goals related to this life-time; actual practice, which is more important than learning; and bodhicitta, which is more important than any other spiritual achievement. Therefore, put these into practice.

**Do not misconstrue.**

Misguided patience is being unable to bear suffering connected with Dharma practice, but able to bear everyday worldy suffering.

Misguided resolve is lacking the aspiration to practice Dharma, but aspiring to carry out activities connected to this life.

Misguided taste is not having a taste for the Dharma, but having a taste for the things of this world.

སྡིག་པ་བྱེད་པ་ལ་སྙིང་རྗེ་མི་སྒོམ་པར་ཆོས་ཕྱིར་དཀའ་བ་སྤྱོད་པ་ལ་སྙིང་རྗེ་སྒོམ་པ་སྙིང་རྗེ་གོ་ལོག  །རང་ལ་ལྟོས་བཅས་ཀྱི་མི་ཆོས་ལ་མི་སྦྱོར་བར་འཇིག་རྟེན་ལ་སྦྱོར་བ་གཉེར་སེམས་གོ་ལོག། གཞན་བདེ་སྐྱིད་ལ་དགའ་བ་མི་སྒོམ་པར་དགྲ་ལ་སྡུག་བསྔལ་བྱུང་ན་དགའ་བ་སྒོམ་པ་ཡི་རང་གོ་ལོག་སྟེ་གོ་ལོག་དྲུག་སྤངས་ནས་གོ་མ་ལོག་པ་དྲུག་ཉམས་སུ་བླང་ངོ་།  །རིས་འཇོག་མི་བྱ༑  ཞེས་པས་ཆོས་ལ་ངེས་ཤེས་མ་སྐྱེས་པས་རིས་བྱེད་པ་འདྲ༑  རིས་མི་བྱེད་པ་འདྲ་དེ་སྤངས་ནས་རྩེ་གཅིག་ཏུ་རྒྱུན་མི་འཆད་པར་བློ་སྦྱང་ངོ་།

Misguided compassion is not practicing compassion towards wrongdoers, but fostering compassion for those who practice austerities in the name of Dharma.

Misguided caring is not encouraging those who depend on us to engage in Dharma-related activities, but encouraging them to do worldly activities.

Misguided rejoicing is not being delighted when others find happiness and joy, but jubilating when enemies experience suffering.

Having rejected the six misconstrued points, practice the six correct ones.

**Do not be inconsistent.**

When conviction in the Dharma fails to develop, sometimes you practice and sometimes you do not. Abandoning this pattern, uninterruptedly and one-pointedly engage in mind training.

དོལ་ཆོད་དུ་སྒྲུང་། ཞེས་པས་བློ་སྦྱོང་ཉིད་ལ་བློ་ཡིངས་ཀྱིས་བསྒྱུར་ནས་ཕྱོགས་གཅིག་ཏུ་སྦྱོང་བའོ། །བརྟགས་དཔྱད་གཉིས་ཀྱིས་ཐར་བར་བྱ། ཞེས་པས་རང་རྒྱུད་ཉོན་མོངས་གང་ཆེ་བརྟགས་ནས། གང་ཆེ་བ་དེ་འབད་པས་སྦྱང་ངོ་། །ཡུས་མ་སྒོམ། ཞེས་པས་ཕ་རོལ་ལ་རང་གི་དྲིན་ཡོད་པ་དང་། རང་གིས་ཆོས་ཡུན་རིང་པོ་བྱས་པ་དང་། མཁས་པ་དང་བརྩུན་པ་ལ་སོགས་པའི་ཡུས་མི་བྱའོ། །ཀོ་ལོང་མ་སྒྲུམ། ཞེས་པ་རང་ལ་གཞན་གྱིས་མི་མང་སར་དམའ་ཕབ་ས་སོགས་ལ་ཀོ་ལོང་མི་བྱ་བའོ། །

**Practice decisively.**

Once your mind has completely surrendered to mind training, make it your only practice.

**Free yourself by examining and analyzing.**

Assess which disturbing emotion dominates your mindstream and make an earnest effort to eliminate it.

**Do not make a habit of showing off.**

Do not boast about being kind to someone; or practicing the Dharma for a long time; or being a scholar or renunciant, and so on.

**Do not be irritable.**

Do not become irritated if, for example, someone offends you in public.

ཡུད་ཙམ་པ་མི་བྱ། ཞེས་པས་ཅུང་ཟད་རེ་ལ་དགའ་མི་དགའི་
རྣམ་འགྱུར་སྟོན་པ་དེ་མི་བྱའོ། །འོར་ཆེ་མ་འདོད། ཅེས་
པས་གཞན་ལ་ཕན་བཏགས་པ་སོགས་ལ་འོར་ཆེ་རེ་བའི་སྣན་
གྲགས་ཀྱི་རེ་བ་མི་བྱའོ། །

## Do not be capricious.

Avoid openly expressing your approval or disapproval of every little thing which occurs.

## Do not crave thanks.

Do not crave the prestige of being thanked if, for instance, you have helped others.

སློགས་མ་ལྷ་པོ་བདོ་བ་འདི། །བྱང་ཆུབ་ལམ་དུ་སྒྱུར་བ་ཡིན། མན་ངག་བདུད་རྩིའི་སྙིང་པོ་འདི། །གསེར་གླིང་པ་ནས་བརྒྱུད་པ་ཡིན། ཞེས་པས་དུས་དང་སེམས་ཅན་དང་ཚེ་དང་ཉོན་མོངས་པ་དང་ལྔ་བའི་སློགས་མ་ལྔ་ལམ་དུ་བསྒྱུར་བའི་ཆོས་ཀྱི་བདུད་རྩིའི། །སྨོན་སྦྱངས་ལས་ཀྱི་འཕྲོ་སད་པས།། རང་གི་མོས་པ་མང་བའི་རྒྱུས། །སྡུག་བསྔལ་གཏམ་ངན་བྲིད་བསད་ནས། །བདག་འཛིན་འདུལ་བའི་གདམས་ངག་ཞུས། །ད་ནི་ཤི་ཡང་མི་འགྱོད་དོ། །ཞེས་པ་ནི་ཆོས་འདི་ལ་དགེ་བའི་བཤེས་གཉེན་འཆད་ཁ་བ་ཉིད་གདེངས་ཐོབ་པའི་གསུང་ངོ་། །ཆོས་ཉམས་ལེན་ཅིག་བྱེད་ན་འདི་ལ་བྱེད་དགོས་པར་གདའོ། །ཞེས་པ་ཞྭ་དམར་པ་ལྷ་པས་ཉམས་ལེན་མདོར་བསྡུས་སུ་བཀོད་པའོ།། །།

*Belonging to the transmission of Serlingpa,*
*this is the essence of the elixir of pith instructions.*
*When the five degenerations are gaining ground*
*it transforms them into the path of awakening.*

This is the Elixir of Dharma which transforms the five degenerations–time, living beings, lifespan, emotional afflictions, and views–into the path.

*When karmic tendencies due to past training were rekindled,*
*I was so deeply inspired that it led me to request*
*–with utter disregard for suffering and defamation–*
*the oral instructions which subdue self-clinging.*
*Were I to die this instant, I would have no regrets.*

Spiritual Friend Chekawa expresses his absolute confidence in this Dharma teaching with these words. If there is just one kind of Dharma to be practiced, it should be this.

This concise explanation of the practice was composed by the fifth Shamarpa.

Translator's note: In the explanation of the slogan **Place these two on the breath**, p. 13, our version of the original text, written in Tibetan umé script, has རླུང་ཚུར་རྔུབ་དུས་སེམས་ཅན་གྱི་བདེ་སྡུག་རང་ལ་ཐིམ། *Meditate that when you breathe in, the happiness and pain of beings dissolve into you.* Our editors suspect that བདེ་སྡུག–*happiness and pain*–is most likely a spelling mistake and should be replaced with སྡིག་སྡུག–*negativities and pain.*

39320918R00051

Made in the USA
Middletown, DE
11 January 2017